Positive Thinking Positive Life: 365 Quotes

By Phil Hunter

CONTENTS

INTRODUCTION

Welcome to the Positive Thinking Positive Life 365 Quotes. In this book, you will find 365 quotes broken down into 12 categories covering some of the most important characteristics for living a positive and successful life. You may have picked up this book because you wanted some daily inspiration or you may have been led here after reading my other book, "Positive Thinking Positive Life: The Mindset". Either way, this book of positive quotes is here to inspire you and can be used as a continuation of your decision to create and sustain a positive mindset to help you get ahead in life, whether that is relationships, business or personal development reasons. For those who have not read my other positive thinking book, I help you understand the mindset which allows you to see the world from a positive perspective. A perspective of someone who loves and believes in themselves and someone who does not let negativity rule or control your life and how to be aware of negative behaviour and patterns which you might not even realise you have. I talked about how to overcome these negative patterns and how to change them into positive ones that will benefit and fuel you to change your beliefs and drive you to greater heights in life by strengthening your character.

"Challenge yourself and you will become stronger and develop character traits that will improve your quality of life and help you achieve success. Qualities such as Humility, Courage, Confidence, Gratefulness, Gratitude, Selflessness, Honesty and Persistence to name but a few. By thinking positively through knowing you can achieve and develop yourself, you are showing self-belief and self-love."

Whether you are trying to get over negative habits, you want the courage to make that decision to travel or open a business, you want to acknowledge and get over your fears, or you simply want some daily inspiration, there is something here for everyone. Each chapter is dedicated to a certain characteristic and I will talk about why it is important and give you some examples of how this will benefit you. It will help you get the fuel to sail your ship into distant, unexplored lands (those who have read my book will understand that one). I will give you around 30 quotes per chapter to use how you like. You might use it for daily inspiration or read certain chapters when you are facing certain challenges in life and want to be inspired or to overcome negativity or fear. How you use it is up to you, but the quotes in the book come from some of the greatest minds in human history and through their works, achievements and mindset, we too can learn the characteristics, traits and qualities and be inspired by the wisdom of some of the greatest minds in history and be grateful for the lessons they have bestowed upon us through their own journey.

It should be one of your goals in life to understand the mindset to see the world from a higher paradigm, a perspective of someone who loves and believes in themselves and someone who does not let negativity rule or control their life. You must love yourself enough to want the best for yourself. To achieve, conquer and strive to reach your potential. I once heard that there are three sorts of individuals in life: those that ignore it, those that watch it and those that get it done. Make, beyond any doubt, you are the person who gets things done. Take control and responsibility for your life and never blame others for where you are. You are in control. You have the power to make the decisions and to decide what journey you will have. Hopefully this book of quotes will help inspire you on your journey.

Positivity and self-belief is an unstoppable force once you harness a positive mindset. It will allow you to become more confident and skilled at facing and solving your problems. You will create and build that positivity and self-belief through changing your thinking patterns which will in turn allow you to become more powerful and successful while also remaining humble and grateful for the journey you are on. It all starts from how you think about yourself and the internal dialogue that you have, so use the information and quotes in this book to reinforce your positive mindset and improve the internal dialogue that have with yourself. If you change how you perceive yourself, through your positive mindset, you will change how you perceive the outside world.

"If there is no enemy within, the enemy outside can do us no harm"

Character is something that is developed over time through the habits of our decisions. If you want to be successful and live a positive and productive life, you must develop yourself through the development of your character. Throughout civilised history, the importance of character and virtue has been pervasive in almost every civilised culture, but most origins can be traced back to the wisdom of the Greeks in an age of philosophical enlightenment and study. Plato, who lived in the fourth century B.C, identified four virtues that have become influential concepts in Western civilization. Now known as the four cardinal virtues, they are prudence (wisdom), temperance (moderation), fortitude (courage) and justice. He wrote about these virtues in the "Republic", a

Socratic dialogue on political theory. Aristotle, a student of Plato, then came up with the term "ethics" in his studies which furthered the idea of virtues by emphasising the importance of behaviour and acting upon these virtues, declaring that a virtuous person is someone who has ideal character traits. He said for a person to become virtuous, he cannot simply study what virtue is, but must do virtuous things. Or if you want me to quote him directly,

"We are not studying in order to know what virtue is, but to become good, for otherwise there would be no profit in it" - (Nicromachean Ethics: Book II)

Other philosophers have argued that the four virtues provide the basis for all aspects of moral character. The virtues were later expanded through the inclusion of additional virtues, such as theologians, who added the three theological virtues: faith, hope and love, which they argue come from the grace of God. Why am I giving you a lesson on Greek and theological philosophy? To highlight the importance of virtues and more importantly being virtuous through our actions which creates the habits of people of highly successful and positive people. All great, successful or influential people, from Plato to Bill Gates, have all behaved and acted in a way that emulates these habits and virtues. If you want to be great, successful, influential or even just get a little further in life, through relationships, personal development or business, I suggest you place importance on virtues, behaviour and traits and learn and understand about each one and what they really mean and the impact they can have on your life.

Further to this, the emphasis is on practicing these virtues and behaviours through habit and repetition. This is what will catapult you towards your own dreams and goals. I say catapult for dramatic effect, but slow progress is still progress, so practicing them daily will slowly, over time, change your character which in turn will move you towards your goals. So depending on how much you want to improve and how much you start practicing it will determine how quickly you progress. People want things too fast, it's an instant gratification culture, so I just want to remind you of the importance of patience and diligence in today's culture. Never be disheartened by not getting results straight away. The greatest rewards come from that feeling of satisfaction after achieving results over prolonged periods of time, effort, patience and hard work. Things such as creating a business or meaningful and lasting relationship, whether that is with your lover, relatives or friends. You will learn more about what I mean as we progress, but the point to note here is don't be afraid to keep coming back to this book or to keep coming back to practicing the positive mindset and lifestyle, even if you fall off the track for a while. If you give up for a while or forget about it, it's okay, you can always pick up where you left off and reignite the fire in your own journey. We only fail when we stop trying.

I hope this book helps you along your journey as learning these things have helped me on mine.

VISION

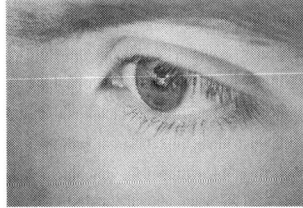

I'm putting this one first because it is the ultimate building block of change. To have the superpower of vision; to visualize where you want to be and what you want is the very first step in achieving anything. The strength and clarity of your vision will determine the elasticity of it and the speed at which you are drawn to it and it is drawn to you. Nothing great was ever achieved without vision. Top level athletes all have this clarity of vision and if you study any of them you will see this for yourself. The ability to visualize can be developed through practice, habit and writing down your ultimate vision for your life. This superpower is not only for the gifted few, it is something you can learn yourself. Yes, some people develop this from an early age, but if someone else has it, it means it can be learnt which means you can learn it too.

A few of my own inspirations in life have had this great superpower, so I will use them as examples to illustrate what vision is and how it is developed. Arnold Schwarzenegger, for example, started weight training at 15. He put posters all over his room of current world champions where he would *visualize* competing and beating them some day. The first thing he looked at and thought about when he woke up and the last thing he looked at and thought about *every single day* was his goals and what he had to do to achieve these goals. No doubt it was on his mind constantly throughout the day too. Your focus determines your reality. By age 20 he had won Mr Universe and by 23 he won Mr Olympia, the youngest ever person to win Mr Olympia.

Conor McGregor, another inspiration of mine, mainly because of his mindset, has this clarity of vision too. Right back from his early professional fights before the UFC there is a video of him saying, "without a doubt you will see me in the UFC". His visualization, which he still uses today, of how he is going to win fights and predicting how (something the legendary Muhammad Ali used to do in boxing also) is something that is backed up by hours of labour in the gym, visualising and preparing for every single contingent. He visualizes every single possible outcome and prepares for it, making sure that nothing is left to chance and he knows how to deal with every possible situation and scenario. Right from the morning of the fight, to him in the dressing room, to walking into the ring, everything has been visualised and that is why he is so comfortable in every situation, because he has lived it many times over in his head. Confidence is simply knowing what to do through experience and practice, something else I will touch on later. I'm not even a big fight fan, I just admire him for his mindset and I study his mentality and his ability to visualize his goals so clearly.

Some people do this visualization naturally but others, like myself, must burn this type of behaviour into my mind by rewriting my goals down on paper every single day and by carrying my main overall goal (encompassing all my goals in one concise statement) on a separate laminated card and carrying it around with me everywhere I go. Daily goal number one for me is always "Vision", which reminds me to spend time visualizing in extreme detail what I have and where I will be. I do it with as much detail as possible, the colour of the car I

10

have, the clothes I am wearing, the emotions I feel as I get out of the car, the emotions I get when I help my family, the type of house I have and the money in my account. After I have spent time on visualizing my dream I will look at the goals I worked out in how to achieve this or at least move me forward in that direction. But it all starts with vision.

Bob Proctor, another inspiration of mine and a fantastic self-development teacher, has carried around the book of his own inspiration, a book by Napoleon Hill, for over 50 years. This book helps him still to visualize his goals and is a constant reminder on the power of positive thinking. Everyone who is successful in life all have the trait of being able to visualize *clearly* what they want and from that, it will begin to manifest into their life, just as the things I am visualizing daily are manifesting into my own life. The more I learnt about vision, the more I became aware of the types of thoughts I had, because the things I think about the most is where I am drawn to. That's why visualising and dreaming about what you want is the first step in achieving it. Think negative and you will get negative results. Think positive and you will get positive results. Visualize daily, visualize often and visualize in detail. The bigger the dream the better and the quicker you will be drawn to it so the faster you will progress. Vision the first step to successful progression and achievement.

"Whatever the mind of man can conceive and believe, it can achieve"

Napoleon Hill

"When I dare to be powerful to use my strength in the service of my vision, then it becomes less and less important whether I am afraid"

Audre Lorde

"In order to carry a positive action, we must develop here a positive vision"

Dalai Lama

"If you can dream it, you can do it"

Walt Disney

"Whatever you can do or dream you can, begin it. Boldness has genius, and magic and power in it. Begin it now"

Goethe

"The greatest danger for most of us is not that our aim is too high and we miss it, but that it is too low and we reach it"

Michelangelo

"Your vision will become clear only when you look into your heart. Who looks outside, dreams. Who looks inside awakens"

Carl Jung

"If you want to build a ship, don't herd people together to collect wood and don't assign them tasks and work, but rather teach them to long for the endless immensity of the sea"

Antoine de Saint-Exupery

"Vision is the art of seeing things invisible"

Jonathan Swift

"Management has a lot to do with answers. Leadership is a function of questions. And the first question for a leader always is: 'Who do we intend to be?' Not 'What are we going to do?' but 'Who do we intend to be?'

Max DePree

"Vision without action is a daydream. Action with without vision is a nightmare"

Japanese Proverb

13

"The best way to predict the future is to create it"

Alan Kay

"Where there is no vision the people perish"

Proverbs 9:8

"Vision without execution is hallucination"

Thomas Edison

"Leadership is the capacity to translate vision into reality"

Warren Bennis

"If you limit your choices only to what seems possible or
reasonable, you disconnect yourself from what you truly want,
and all that is left is a compromise"

Robert Fritz

"Create your future from your future, not your past"

Werner Erhard

"To the person who does not know where he wants to go there is no favourable wind"

Seneca

"You've got to think about big things while you're doing small things, so that all the small things go in the right direction"

Alvin Toffler

"To accomplish great things, we must dream as well as act"

Anatole France

"A leader's role is to raise people's aspirations for what they can become and to release their energies so they will try to get there"

David Gergen

"The very essence of leadership is that you have a vision. It's got to be a vision you articulate clearly and forcefully on every occasion. You can't blow an uncertain trumpet"

Theodore Hesburgh

"Determine that the thing can and shall be done and then we shall find the way"

Abraham Lincoln

"Cherish your visions and your dreams as they are the children of your soul, the blueprints of your ultimate achievements"

Napoleon Hill

"Pain pushes until vision pulls"

Michael Beckwith

"Vision animates, inspires, transforms purpose into action"

Warren Bennis

"The master of the art of living makes little distinction between his work and his play, his labour and his leisure, his mind and his body, his education and his recreation, his love and his religion. He hardly knows which is which; he simply pursues his vision of excellence in whatever he does, leaving others to decide whether he is working or playing. To him he is always doing both"

Buddha

"Rowing harder doesn't help if the boat is headed in the wrong direction"

Kenichi Ohmae

"It's not what the vision is, it's what the vision does"

Peter Senge

"In the business world, the rear-view mirror is always clearer than the windshield"

Warren Buffett

"A leader will find it difficult to articulate a coherent vision unless it expresses his core values, his basic identity. One must first embark on the formidable journey of self-discovery in order to create a vision with authentic soul"

Mihaly Csikszentmihalyi

"You have to know what you want. And if it seems to take you off the track, don't hold back, because perhaps that is instinctively where you want to be. And if you hold back and try to be always where you have been before, you will go dry"

Gertrude Stein

"The gift of fantasy has meant more to me than my talent for absorbing positive knowledge"

Albert Einstein

"I try to learn from the past, but I plan for the future by focusing exclusively on the present. That's where the fun is"

Donald Trump

"The most pathetic person in the world is someone who has sight, but has no vision"

Helen Keller

"Good business leaders create a vision, articulate the vision, passionately own the vision, and relentlessly drive it to completion"

Jack Welsh

"A vision is not just a picture of what could be; it is an appeal to our better selves, a call to become something more"

Rosabeth Moss Kanter

"If I have seen farther than others, it is because I was standing on the shoulders of giants"

Isaac Newton

"The future belongs to those who see possibilities before they become obvious"

John Scully

"If one advances confidently in the direction of his dreams, and endeavours to live the life which he has imagined, he will meet with success unexpected in common hours"

Henry David Thoreau

"Keep your eyes on the stars and your feet on the ground"

Franklin D. Roosevelt

"Looking up gives light, although at first it makes you dizzy"

Rumi

"You cannot depend on your eyes when your imagination is out of focus"

Mark Twain

"In order to be a realist, you must believe in miracles"

David BenGurion

"The real voyage of discovery consists of not in seeking new landscapes but in having new eyes"

Marcel Proust

FEAR

The blockage of progress. The silent killer of vision. The keeper of mediocrity. The mass murderer of dreams. Everyone knows that fear holds you back, but not everyone fully understands the impact this really has on our lives. I know what fear is, but I also dedicate a lot of my time to understanding it and constantly remind myself of how it can make decisions for me if I let it. Fear brings anxiety, stress, discomfort, pain. Does fear ever go away? The sad answer is no. It will always be there. It is an extremely strong impulse that has been hardwired into us through evolution so that we can survive. That is why it is so strong, it has allowed us to get to where we are today in terms or the survival of the human race. The thing is, because it is so prominent in our psychology most people entertain these fears because it is easier to give in to them and keep the status quo.

Fear can raise its ugly head in many forms. Some are obvious such as the sheer terror experienced when jumping off the top diving board as a kid, or jumping out of a plane skydiving for the first time, or asking out your crush when you were a child. Other forms of fear are more subtle and cloaked, such as forms of scepticism, doubt and disbelief. Sometimes those subtle forms appear in your internal dialogue, the minds way of trying to talk you out of doing something too risky and trying to keep you to your old habits. It comes in the guise of rational thought or intellectual criticism. These intellectual faculties are very important to have, but it is also wise to see the limits these kinds of faculties can have in decision making and progression. Should I have my doubts and scepticism that I can open a big and successful business, yes. Should I allow this doubt and scepticism to stop me from conquering my fear of failure and embarrassment, no. More importantly, should I allow the doubts and scepticism of others to seep into my own beliefs and dissuade me from following my own dreams... hell no.

That's why it is so important to listen to nobody else but yourself. People will talk you right out of going after your goals. The bigger your dreams, the more resistance you are going to get from others. Surround yourself by the small percentage of like-minded people that are taking the big risks themselves. For every 100 people in your life, only about 3 of them will be the type of people to encourage you to dream big and go after your goals without letting fear affect your decisions because that is what they had to do in their life. Surround yourself with that 3%.

Repetition Is a definitive concept when learning any new habits such as decision making and getting over fear. Your mind does not want to change, it wants to maintain the status quo. Whenever you have new habits, your mind will try to bring you back to the original habits because it's safe. That's why they say you need to practice and implement habits daily, repeat them at least 3 times a day for 90 days before it becomes your new habit, otherwise you will revert to your default habits. Tony Robbins will talk about momentum, starting small and building up this momentum into big habits. Bob Proctor talks about the paradigm and why you must change your paradigm to change your behaviour and habits. I like to think about it as pushing a boulder up a hill. If you push the boulder half way up the hill and you stop, it will roll back down to the bottom again. But if keep pushing that boulder until you reach the top of the hill, there it will stay forever. You must keep the habit and momentum up until the point that the habit has become part of who you are.

Part of overcoming fears is therefore your repetition of action towards those fears and the decisions you make despite them. Fear never truly goes away, but what you can do is learn to understand its many forms and then embrace and acknowledge that fear and see it as an opportunity for growth and to overcome it through practicing traits like courage and persistence. You will learn to become aware of the limits in your thinking and by making decisions to face your fears, with time, you will see fear as a good thing because it is an opportunity for improving yourself. You can turn the negative energy of fear into a positive one by realising that fear is an opportunity. It is where you will challenge yourself and grow. Learn to crash through those terror barriers as Bob Proctor puts it and you will find a life of freedom, prosperity and wealth.

"The cave you fear to enter holds the treasure you seek"

Joseph Campbell

"People living deeply have no fear of death"

Anais Nin

"When a resolute young fellow steps up to the great bully, the world, and takes him boldly by the beard, he is often surprised to find it comes off in his hand, and that it was only tied on to scare away the timid adventurers"

Ralph Waldo Emerson

"Fear is the main source of superstition, and one of the main sources of cruelty. To conquer fear is the beginning of wisdom"

Bertrand Russell

"Fears are educated into us, and can, if we wish, be educated out"

Karl Augustus Menninger

"Curiosity will conquer fear even more than bravery will"

James Stephens

"I must not fear.
Fear is the mind-killer.
Fear is the little-death that brings total obliteration.
I will face my fear.
I will permit it to pass over me and through me.
And when it has gone past I will turn the inner eye to see its path.

Where the fear has gone there will be nothing.
Only I will remain"

Frank Herbert

"Fear: False Evidence Appearing Real"

Unknown

"I am not afraid of tomorrow, for I have seen yesterday and I love today"

William Allen White

"Who sees all beings in his own self, and his own self in all beings, loses all fear"

Isa Upanishad, Hindu Scripture

"Where no hope is left, is left no fear"

Milton

"Fear is only as deep as the mind allows"

Japanese Proverb

"Avoiding danger is no safer in the long run than outright exposure. The fearful are caught as often as the bold"

Helen Keller

"You can discover what your enemy fears most by observing the means he uses to frighten you"

Eric Hoffer

"If you are distressed by anything external, the pain is not due to the thing itself, but to your estimate of it; and this you have the power to revoke at any moment"

Marcus Aurelius

"When I hear music, I fear no danger. I am invulnerable. I see no foe. I am related to the earliest times, and to the latest"

Henry David Thoreau

"You gain strength, courage, and confidence by every experience in which you really stop to look fear in the face. You must do the thing which you think you cannot do"

Eleanor Roosevelt

"In skating over thin ice our safety is in our speed"

Ralph Waldo Emerson

"The oldest and strongest emotion of mankind is fear, and the oldest and strongest kind of fear is fear of the unknown"

H.P Lovecraft

"Inaction breeds doubt and fear. Action breeds confidence and courage. If you want to conquer fear, do not sit home and think about it. Go out and get busy"

Dale Carnegie

"Try a thing you haven't done three times. Once, to get over the fear of doing it. Twice, to learn how to do it. And a third time to figure out whether you like it or not"

Virgil Thomson

"The enemy is fear. We think it is hate; but, it is fear"

Gandhi

"Never be afraid to try something new. Remember, amateurs built the ark, professionals built the Titanic"

Unknown

23

COURAGE

Courage is defined by the Oxford dictionary as: "the ability to do something that frightens one; bravery". In the last chapter, I mentioned that fear can be an opportunity for growth. If you want to look at it from another angle is that fear gives us the opportunity to be courageous. Marie Curie for example, struggled with an ongoing battle against the sexism of the time and was constantly challenged on her scientific career and her choice to give up sexist stereotypes, which at the time, was the ideal that woman should stay at home to take care of the children while the men had careers and worked, providing the income, while the woman stayed at home as a permanent house keeper to raise the children. It was only through her consistent courage of going against the ideals of the time that she was able to succeed in great scientific as well as feminist achievements. She became the first woman to ever receive a Nobel Prize in 1903 for her achievements in science. Those that want to succeed in life must be courageous and willing to stand up for what they believe.

There are many forms of bravery, from jumping over the trenches when face the enemy, to asking your boss for a raise, or even to stand up to the social and political norms of the times, such as the case of Marie Curie. There are many different forms, but they are all important and can impact the lives of not only yourself, but of the people around you. By not following your own inner voice, you are deflating your self-image and character. Shakespeare said in Julius Caesar,

"A coward dies a thousand times before his death, but the valiant taste of death but once. It seems to me most strange that men should fear, seeing that death, a necessary end, will come when it will come".

What Shakespeare is saying here is that those who do not face their fears or run from them, will die a little inside until their own inner strength diminishes and their soul weakens. The strength of character and verve will weaken and you will lose your sense of identity. The human spirit, which is identity of a greater ideal and the foundation of everything that the human race stands for, will diminish. Those that have the courage to face their fears will only die once, which would be their physical death when their time comes. Seek to strengthen your character by overcoming fear through courage. The word itself comes from the French "corage" meaning heart, innermost feelings, temper. Learn to follow your heart. If you listen closely, it will tell you what you need to do, but listen careful because most of the time, it whispers.

The rewards from listening to your inner voice and acting on it is indescribable, you will reach your goals and improve your character exponentially from overcoming the silent killer of dreams, fear. Like the kickboxing fights I took when I was young, it scared the hell out of me but that is exactly why I done it. The confidence and sense of pride and achievement I got from this was indescribable. When opportunity comes for me now, I know to acknowledge my fears but act despite them. It never goes away but I turn that negative energy into positive ones and see it as an opportunity to be brave and test my grit.

Other forms of courage, like Marie Curie, is the ability to speak your truth in the face of conformity and opposition or to stand up to adversity. It allows you to shine and become a greater version of yourself. Another way you can be courageous is to carry on despite failure, no matter how big or how consistent that failure is. Like Thomas Edison who failed to create the lightbulb a thousand times, he had the courage to continue until he succeeded. Courage is a character trait of all great men, women and achievers throughout history. Learn to embrace courage in its many forms and seek to expand the human spirit through facing adversity.

"It takes a great deal of bravery to stand up to our enemies, but just as much to stand up to our friends"

J.K Rowling, Harry Potter and the Sorcerer's Stone

"Being deeply loved by someone gives you strength, while loving someone deeply gives you courage"

Lao Tzu

"Success is not final, failure is not fatal: it is the courage to continue that counts"

Winston S. Churchill

"It takes courage to grow up and become who you really are"

E.E Cummings

"I wanted you to see what real courage is, instead of getting the idea that courage is a man with a gun in his hand. It's when you know you're licked before you begin, but you begin anyway and see it through no matter what
Atticus Finch"

Harper Lee, To Kill a Mockingbird

"The most courageous act is still to think for yourself. Aloud"

Coco Chanel

"Above all, be the heroine of your life, not the victim"

Nora Ephron

"Bran thought about it. 'Can a man still be brave if he's afraid?' 'That is the only time a man can be brave,' his father told him"

George R.R Martin, A Game of Thrones

"Courage is the most important of all the virtues because without courage, you can't practice any other virtue consistently"

Maya Angelou

"You cannot swim for new horizons until you have courage to lose sight of the shore"

William Faulkner

"Everyone has talent. What's rare is the courage to follow it to the dark places where it leads"

Erica Jong

"Don't be afraid of your fears. They're not there to scare you. They're there to let you know that something is worth it"

C. JoyBell C.

"Confront the dark parts of yourself, and work to banish them with illumination and forgiveness. Your willingness to wrestle with your demons will cause your angels to sing"

August Wilson

"Have enough courage to trust love one more time and always one more time"

Maya Angelou

"There is a stubbornness about me that never can bear to be frightened at the will of others. My courage always rises at every attempt to intimidate me"

Jane Austen, Pride and Prejudice

"A ship is safe in harbour, but that's not what ships are for"

William G.T Shedd

"Life shrinks or expands in proportion to one's courage"

Anaïs Nin

"Don't be satisfied with stories, how things have gone with others. Unfold your own myth"

Jalaluddin Rumi, The Essential Rumi

"Scared is what you're feeling. Brave is what you're doing"

Emma Donoghue, Room

"Courage is resistance to fear, mastery of fear, not absence of fear"

Mark Twain

"For what it's worth: it's never too late or, in my case, too early to be whoever you want to be There's no time limit, stop whenever you want You can change or stay the same, there are no rules to this thing We can make the best or the worst of it I hope you make the best of it And I hope you see things that startle you I hope you feel things you never felt before I hope you meet people with a different point of view I hope you live a life you're proud of If you find that you're not, I hope you have the courage to start all over again"

Eric Roth, The Curious Case of Benjamin Button Screenplay

"When we least expect it, life sets us a challenge to test our courage and willingness to change; at such a moment, there is no point in pretending that nothing has happened or in saying that we are not yet ready. The challenge will not wait. Life does not look back. A week is more than enough time for us to decide whether or not to accept our destiny"

Paulo Coelho, The Devil and Miss Prym

"There are so many ways to be brave in this world. Sometimes bravery involves laying down your life for something bigger than yourself, or for someone else. Sometimes it involves giving up everything you have ever known, or everyone you have ever loved, for the sake of something greater. But sometimes it doesn't. Sometimes it is nothing more than gritting your teeth through pain, and the work of every day, the slow walk toward a better life. That is the sort of bravery I must have now"

Veronica Roth, Allegiant

"Courage is found in unlikely places"

J.R.R Tolkien

"With enough courage, you can do without a reputation"

Margaret Mitchell

"All happiness depends on courage and work"

Honoré de Balzac

"I learned that courage was not the absence of fear, but the triumph over it. The brave man is not he who does not feel afraid, but he who conquers that fear"

Nelson Mandela

"The two hardest tests on the spiritual road are the patience to wait for the right moment and the courage not to be disappointed with what we encounter"

Paulo Coelho, Veronika Decides to Die

"Freedom lies in being bold"

Robert Frost

"We can't be afraid of change. You may feel very secure in the pond that you are in, but if you never venture out of it, you will never know that there is such a thing as an ocean, a sea. Holding onto something that is good for you now, may be the very reason why you don't have something better"

C.JoyBell C

SELF-BELIEF

Everything stems from Self-belief. Nothing is ever achieved without it. Allow yourself the imagination to create a vision for your life and hold it in your mind. Then write down your vision and have the courage to believe that somewhere inside yourself is the strength and potential to overcome the adversity along the way. The self-belief will be the catalyst for change. Positivity and self-belief are an unstoppable force once you harness the positive mindset. It will allow you to become more confident and skilled at facing and solving your problems. You will create and build that positivity and self-belief through changing your thinking patterns which will in turn allow you to become more powerful and successful. It all starts from how you think about yourself and the internal dialogue that you have. If you change how you perceive yourself, through the positive mindset, you will change how you perceive the outside world. Love and respect yourself enough to want to change and this will determine your choices and actions. You should achieve your goals or dreams while remaining grateful, humble and appreciative of what you have. With self-belief, there is a world of possibilities out there, nothing is unachievable. Elon Musk takes this to a whole new level and is the pinnacle of what we should aspire to become.

His self-belief is ridiculously crazy and something that we should emulate. The things that he has achieved all started with his own self-belief. This is backed up with hard work and courageousness to continue forward despite his failures, among other things, but the runners starter block for his achievements was self-belief.

Self-belief is the ultimate form of love, because if you can't love yourself then you cannot love others and therefore you cannot help them or make a positive change in their lives too. For those who have read my other book, you will know that this belief is all learnable and through praxis (the practical application of the knowledge) you can build up this self-belief and the doors of opportunity start opening everywhere. Avoid self-doubt it all costs, become aware of the positive and negative around you and be very careful what you let into your thoughts. Extinguish the doubt and fears from your thought patterns and invest in yourself. Invest in the belief of your inner potential and become aware through time of your own greatness. The words "inner potential" can come across as vague or cliché, but I highly suggest you learn what this term really means and how to achieve it through action. Become great.

Negativity is all around us in the news, radio, friends, family and the internet, which all bombard us. It is so important to our success to be aware of this negativity and how it can influence your thoughts in terms of increasing self-doubt, scepticism, fear and disbelief. Your thoughts create your actions and behaviour, and as you learn about self-belief, you begin to nurture and protect it like it's your own child. Spoiler alert: it is your own child. It's what people refer to as your inner child, which is really just a metaphor for the creative, fun-loving, curious and optimistic young child that you once were. Think of how that child looked at everything with wonder, novelty and imagination, which allowed you to have fun and experience laughter and excitement. Don't let others drown it out. Embrace that little ball of goodness called your inner child that you have inside yourself. It will take you places. Focus on building up your self-belief through courage, doing things that you love and setting yourself challenges. When you start succeeding in challenges (even if it takes a few failures first), then your self-esteem and confidence in yourself will rise and feed of that momentum to see where it can take you.

"Love yourself first and everything else falls into line. You really have to love yourself to get anything done in this world"

Lucille Ball

"You yourself, as much as anybody in the entire universe, deserve your love and affection"

Buddha

"Until you value yourself, you won't value your time. Until you value your time, you will not do anything with it"

M. Scott Peck

"A man cannot be comfortable without his own approval"

Mark Twain

"Never be bullied into silence. Never allow yourself to be made a victim. Accept no one's definition of your life, but define yourself"

Harvey Fierstein

"Remember always that you not only have the right to be an individual, you have an obligation to be one"

Eleanor Roosevelt

"If only you could sense how important you are to the lives of those you meet; how important you can be to people you may never even dream of. There is something of yourself that you leave at every meeting with another person"

Fred Rogers

"Low self-esteem is like driving through life with your hand break on"

Maxwell Maltz

"What lies behind us and what lies before us are tiny matters compared to what lies within us"

Ralph Waldo Emerson

"When you recover or discover something that nourishes your soul and brings joy, care enough about yourself to make room for it in your life"

Jean Shinoda Bolen

"Selfcare is never a selfish act—it is simply good stewardship of the only gift I have, the gift I was put on earth to offer to others"

Parker Palmer

"When you adopt the viewpoint that there is nothing that exists that is not part of you, that there is no one who exists who is not part of you, that any judgment you make is self-judgment, that any criticism you level is self-criticism, you will wisely extend to yourself an unconditional love that will be the light of the world"

Harry Palmer

"Why should we worry about what others think of us, do we have more confidence in their opinions than we do our own?"

Brigham Young

"To establish true self-esteem, we must concentrate on our successes and forget about the failures and the negatives in our lives"

Denis Waitley

"A healthy selflove means we have no compulsion to justify to ourselves or others why we take vacations, why we sleep late, why we buy new shoes, why we spoil ourselves from time to time. We feel comfortable doing things which add quality and beauty to life"

Andrew Matthews

"Our self-respect tracks our choices. Every time we act in harmony with our authentic self and our heart, we earn our respect. It is that simple. Every choice matters"

Dan Coppersmith

"People may flatter themselves just as much by thinking that their faults are always present to other people's minds, as if they believe that the world is always contemplating their individual charms and virtues"

Elizabeth Gaskell

"Don't rely on someone else for your happiness and self-worth. Only you can be responsible for that. If you can't love and respect yourself no one else will be able to make that happen. Accept who you are completely; the good and the bad and make changes as YOU see fit not because you think someone else wants you to be different"

Stacey Charter

"Don't ask yourself what the world needs, ask yourself what makes you come alive. And then go and do that. Because what the world needs is people who have come alive"

Howard Washington Thurman

"Too many people overvalue what they are not and undervalue what they are"

Malcolm S. Forbes

"Whatever course you decide upon, there is always someone to tell you that you are wrong. There are always difficulties arising which tempt you to believe that your critics are right. To map out a course of action and follow it to an end requires courage"

Ralph Waldo Emerson

"Never bend your head. Always hold it high Look the world straight in the face"

Helen Keller

"You have been criticizing yourself for years, and it hasn't worked. Try approving of yourself and see what happens"

Louise L. Hay

"To love oneself is the beginning of a lifelong romance"

Oscar Wilde

"Be faithful to that which exists within yourself"

André Gide

"Act as if what you do makes a difference. It does"

William James

"The most beautiful people we have known are those who have known defeat, known suffering, known struggle, known loss, and have found their way out of the depths. These persons have an appreciation, a sensitivity and an understanding of life that fills them with compassions, gentleness, and a deep loving concern. Beautiful people do not just happen"

Elizabeth Kubler-Ross

"You're always with yourself, so you might as well enjoy the company"

Diane Von Furstenberg

"Who looks outside, dreams; who looks inside, awakes"

Carl Gustav Jung

"No one can make you feel inferior without your consent"

Eleanor Roosevelt

"The better you feel about yourself, the less you feel the need to show off"

Robert Hand

"I think everybody's weird. We should all celebrate our individuality and not be embarrassed or ashamed of it"

Johnny Depp

"You are very powerful, provided you know how powerful you are"

Yogi Bhajan

"It ain't what they call you, it's what you answer to"

W.C. Fields

"There are days I drop words of comfort on myself like falling leaves and remember that it is enough to be taken care of by myself"

Brian Andreas

"Trust yourself. You know more than you think you do"

Benjamin Spock

"Because one believes in oneself, one doesn't try to convince others. Because one is content with oneself, one doesn't need others' approval. Because one accepts oneself, the whole world accepts him or her"

Lao Tzu

"People who want the most approval get the least and the people who need approval the least get the most"

Wayne Dyer

"There is nothing noble about being superior to some other man. The true nobility is in being superior to your previous self"

Hindu Proverb

"I found in my research that the biggest reason people aren't more self-compassionate is that they are afraid they'll become self-indulgent. They believe self-criticism is what keeps them in line. Most people have gotten it wrong because our culture says being hard on yourself is the way to be"

Kristen Neff

"Your problem is you're… too busy holding onto your unworthiness"

Ram Dass

"The reward for conformity is that everyone likes you but yourself"

Rita Mae Brown

"She lacks confidence, she craves admiration insatiably. She lives on the reflections of herself in the eyes of others. She does not dare to be herself"

Anais Nin

"People are like stained-glass windows. They sparkle and shine when the sun is out, but when the darkness sets in their true beauty is revealed only if there is light from within"

Elisabeth Kübler-Ross

"If you aren't good at loving yourself, you will have a difficult time loving anyone, since you'll resent the time and energy you give another person that you aren't even giving to yourself"

Barbara De Angelis

"Most of the shadows of this life are caused by standing in one's own sunshine"

Ralph Waldo Emerson

"It's surprising how many persons go through life without ever recognizing that their feelings toward other people are largely determined by their feelings toward themselves, and if you're not comfortable within yourself, you can't be comfortable with others"

Sidney J. Harris

"There came a time when the risk to remain tight in the bud was more painful than the risk it took to blossom"

Anais Nin

"It took me a long time not to judge myself through someone else's eyes"

Sally Field

"When I loved myself enough, I began leaving whatever wasn't healthy. This meant people, jobs, my own beliefs and habits anything that kept me small   My judgement called it disloyal. Now I see it as self-loving"

Kim McMillen

"The best day of your life is the one on which you decide your life is your own. No apologies or excuses. No one to lean on, rely on, or blame. The gift is yours it is an amazing journey and you alone are responsible for the quality of it. This is the day your life really begins"

Bob Moawad

"Self-pity gets you nowhere. One must have the adventurous daring to accept oneself as a bundle of possibilities and undertake the most interesting game in the world making the most of one's best"

Harry Emerson Fosdick

"It is never too late to be what you might have been"

George Eliot

NEGATIVITY

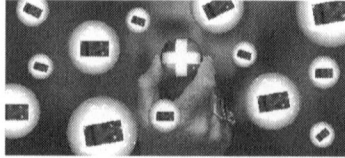

We touched upon negativity in the last chapter and how to be aware of the thoughts you let into your mind because your thoughts determine your behaviour. When you control and are aware of the thoughts you let in, then you start to focus on positive thoughts and being surrounded by positive people. Your behaviour will show in things like how you react and respond to thoughts, events or people. This behaviour ultimately comes from how you perceive the thoughts, events or people internally, which stems from how you perceive yourself. This is very important, so think about this carefully. Reread it if you have to.

When you value and respect yourself, you will always want the best for yourself. In this regard, you will take pride in what you do and how you think. You will never see yourself through the eyes of those who do not value you. You will judge yourself by your own standards, which is that you are a strong powerful being, capable of inspiring others, helping them and caring for those around you. This is fundamental to understanding self-belief and negativity. The higher your belief in yourself, the less negativity you will allow into your thoughts and the less it will affect you. You will have your negativity shield all full power. You can help others that may have negative habits but you will not allow that negativity to affect you, it will bounce of your protective shield and through this you can inspire others through your own positivity and actions.

In my own life, I make a conscious effort to surround myself with positive people, high achievers and people that are aware of the impact of positive and negative thinking on behaviour. I was in a coffee shop earlier with one such person and his level of awareness around this ingredient for success is exactly why I have him in my inner circle. He was very conscious of using the correct words and would correct himself (or me) if he used the wrong type of word. We were sitting there chatting about our goals and he was advising me on tailoring my goals and he used the word realistic. He paused for a second and then said, "I don't like that word, I don't like using it. It's very limiting. The Wright Brothers weren't realistic when they made the decision they were going to fly. Thomas Edison wasn't realistic when he created the lightbulb". It could seem like something trivial to those who aren't aware of the impact of thoughts, but he would be very concise on the words he used and the things he thought. This is the level you must reach when you understand the concept of awareness and the impact of positive and negative thoughts on behaviour and therefore, become almost clinical in your use of thoughts and language.

When you see yourself as a high-value person, you will become internally calm and at peace with yourself, you will perceive things in a passive manner and not take what other people say or do personally because you do not define yourself by the standards of what others think. You will be passive in your response to these situations and you will be able to view the event objectively and you will be able to handle the situation because you have mastered your emotions. Bob Proctor puts it in this way, "When you react, you are giving away your power. When you respond, you are staying in control of yourself".

In terms of negative behaviours from others, a negative attitude or behaviour stems from the protagonist's lack of self-belief and self-respect in themselves. They can try to put others down so they can feed their own ego or make themselves feel better, even if that feeling is short lived (they need that hit of dopamine to boost their low energy). The negative behaviour stems from something that is lacking in their life and it is not aimed at the victim, but rather themselves. With negative situations or environments, it is all in how you perceive those events and how you internally interpret them which stems from how you see yourself. If you find you are very negative about things, try and build up your self-confidence and belief in yourself.

When you learn to overcome negativity, or convert it into positive energy through the right mindset and self-development, then nothing will hold you back. You really can be your own worst enemy but when you learn to conquer yourself and become the hero in your own story and not just an extra, then nothing or nobody will dampen your spirit and remarkable things will begin to happen as you start to unlock your own potential and abilities over time and through dedication to the process of improvement through positive thinking.

"If there is no enemy within, the enemy outside can do us no harm"

African Proverb

"Negativity is the enemy of creativity"

David Lynch

"When someone tells me 'no', it doesn't mean I can't do it, it simply means I can't do it with them"

Karen E Quinones Miller

"Seeing the glass as half empty is more positive than seeing it as half full Through such a lens the only choice is to pour more That is righteous pessimism"

Criss Jami

"Nothing can doom man but the belief in doom, for this prevents the movement of return"

Martin Buber

"Negativity is cannibalistic. The more you feed it, the bigger and stronger it grows"

Bobby Darnell

"A lot of people will ignore positive words when they are down and accept negative words. Those people never get better"

Travis J Dahnke

"People who project negativity typically have low self-esteem
They feel badly about themselves, and their negativity is
simply a reflection of those feelings"

Hendrie Weisinger

"Negativity is an addiction to the bleak shadow that lingers
around every human form. You can transfigure negativity by
turning it toward the light of your soul"

John O'Donohue

"Negativity can only feed on negativity"

Elisabeth KublerRoss

"Sensitive souls draw in the negativity of others because they
are so open"

John Gray

"All negativity is an illusion created by the limited mind to
protect and defend itself"

Ambika Wauters

"Dwelling on the negative simply contributes to its power"

Shirley MacLaine

"To expect defeat is nine tenths of defeat itself"

Francis Crawford

"The greatest griefs are those we cause ourselves"

Sophocles

"Living in the past is a dull and lonely business; looking back strains the neck muscles, and causes you to bump into people not going your way"

Ferber

"The worst loneliness is not to be comfortable with yourself"

Mark Twain

"Forget your sadness, anger, grudges and hatred Let them pass like smoke caught in a breeze Do not indulge yourself in such feelings"

Masaaki Hatsumi

"The heaviest thing I can carry is a grudge"

Unknown

"Some people grumble that roses have thorns; I am grateful that thorns have roses"

Alphonse Karr

"Stop letting people who do so little for you control so much of your mind, feelings and emotions"

Will Smith

"Worry deprives you of strength and makes everything much worse, than what actually is"

Dr Anil Kr Sinha

"Nobody can motivate himself in a positive direction by continually using negative words"

John C Maxwell

"Fear is that little dark room where negatives are developed"

Michael Pritchard

"He who has never hoped, can never despair"

George Bernard Shaw

"The world is round and the place which may seem like the end may also be only the beginning"

George Baker

"If you don't know the struggle, you don't know your strength"

Mary Kay

"The mind acts like an enemy for those who do not control it"

Bhagavad Gita

"Stop allowing other people to dilute or poison your day with their words or opinions"

Steve Maraboli

"There are some people who always seem angry and continuously look for conflict Walk away; the battle they are fighting isn't with you, it is with themselves"

Unknown

"Criticism does not make you smarter or better than the one you are criticizing In fact, the stuff you are critical of in others is the same stuff you don't like about yourself"

Iyanla Vanzant

"I will not let anyone walk through my mind with their dirty feet"

Mahatma Gandhi

"A pessimist is a man who thinks everybody is as nasty as himself, and hates them for it"

George Bernard Shaw

"A pessimist sees the difficulty in every opportunity; an optimist sees the opportunity in every difficulty"

Winston S Churchill

"The more you dwell on what you don't have, the more you get what you don't want"

Unknown

"Insanity: doing the same thing over and over again and expecting different results"

Albert Einstein

"If you accept the expectations of others, especially negative ones, then you never will change the outcome"

Michael Jordan

"The smaller the mind the greater the conceit"

Aesop

"Don't believe in pessimism If something doesn't come up the way you want, forge ahead If you think it's going to rain, it will"

Clint Eastwood

"I feel uncomfortable because I'm insecure about who I am"

Trent Reznor

"Some men have thousands of reasons why they cannot do what they want to, when all they need is one reason why they can"

Martha Graham

"Adopting the right attitude can convert a negative stress into a positive one"

Dr Hans Selye

"However vast the darkness, we must supply our own Light"

Stanley Kubrick

"Keep away from people who try to belittle your ambitions Small people always do that, but the really great make you feel that you, too, can become great"

Mark Twain

"Negative words are powerful boomerangs so be careful what you say about people and yourself"

Mary J Blige

"The cost of living is going up, and the chance of living is going down"

Flip Wilson

"The mass of men lead lives of quiet desperation"

Henry David Thoreau

"The chip on my shoulder's a little heavy I have back problems now"

Janeane Garofalo

"The best way of removing negativity is to laugh and be joyous"

David Icke

"No one can create negativity or stress within you Only you can do that by virtue of how you process your world"

Wayne Dyer

"All negativity is caused by an accumulation of psychological time and denial of the present"

Eckhart Tolle

LOVE

There are many different forms of love and to understand these forms better, just like virtues, we must go back to the age of Classical Greece to discover a little bit more. Classical Greece was the period in history around the 5th and 4th centuries BC where Greek civilisation had a heavy influence on the Roman Empire and therefore the foundations of Western Civilisation. Much of our politics, artistic thought (architecture, sculpture), scientific thought, theatre, literature and philosophy has its roots deeply set in this period of history. This was the time of Socrates, Plato, Xenophon and Aristotle. Just like the virtues, the greatest minds of that time came together, in their search for wisdom, to think deeply about the various topics that affect human civilisation and culture. One of those topics was love, what it is and what it means. The word love can be confusing at times, it can be quite ambiguous, subjective and come in many various levels and forms. In the English language, we only have one word for it. The Greeks, however, in their great wisdom, came up with 8 different words for love, each referring to a different type of love. Let's look at these to delve deeper into this topic of love.

- Eros. Erotic love named after the goddess of fertility and represents the idea of sexual passion and desire.

- Philia. Affectionate and platonic love like friendships. The Greeks valued philia above eros because it was considered a love between equals.

- Storage. Familiar love, similar to philia in that it is a love without physical attraction, but storage is primarily to do with kinship and familiarity, such as the love between parents and children or vice versa (vice versa is also a Latin word literally meaning "the other way around").

- Ludus. Playful love, like that of young lovers experiencing the early stages of a deeper love. Ludus also exists in the deeper forms of love and is actually an ingredient for it. A child-like form of love, which brings fun, excitement and laughter.

- Mania. A destructive type of love which comes from an imbalance between eros and ludus and can lead a person into madness or obsessiveness. Ironically, the way to deal with this type of love is another form of love, philautia. Those that have mania often suffer from low self-esteem. They want to be loved or find their own value through others. They often become obsessed with other people or things and often leads to codependency in relationships.

- Philautia. Self-love. The Greeks understood all those years ago that we must love and care about ourselves first before we can love and care for others. This love is not vain, egotistic, narcissistic or self-obsessed. It is the healthy style of love which is related to self-belief, valuing yourself and your time and being comfortable with who you are as a person and wanting the best for yourself because you understand your own worth. Aristotle said, "All friendly feelings for others are an extension of a man's feeling for himself". You cannot

66

give love if you don't have love inside you first to give. I say fill yourself with self-love/philautia so much that it overflows from you and spills into the world, surrounding everyone around you with love too.

- Pragma. Enduring love that has aged, developed and matured over time. This is found in long term friendships and marriages. It is not easily found and we spend so much time and energy on finding love that we rarely spend time and energy on maintaining that love. Pragma comes from both sides showing compassion, patience and tolerance to make the relationship work.

- Agape. The highest and most regarded form of love to the Greeks. It is a selfless or unconditional love. It is an unconditional love that is bigger than ourselves, a boundless compassion and empathy for other beings. It is a pure form of love that is not selfish or does not desire anything in return. It is forgiveness, acceptance, benevolence, a good will and desire for others. The good will for others to achieve, find self-acceptance and love in their lives with no expectations of anything in return.

Love is a powerful driver and emotion, it comes in many forms. It can be given or received, it can pull us towards something, push us away from someone or motivate us to get to somewhere beyond our reach. Whatever it is you want to do in life, make sure the vision, passion and self-belief are all aligned with a deeper purpose of love, whatever form that may take. Avoid mania and focus on aligning your goals and purpose with philia, storage, ludus, philautia, pragma and agape. Money goals are great and you focus on money, you will get it, but a better idea is focus on the love for your family, friends and partner and how your success can help provide for them.

If you had financial freedom and all the wealth in the world, how would you spend your time? We are all creative beings; so explore this creativity through imagination with your vision and see what you can come up with. Bring this love into your vision by including your family, friends and partners and what you can provide for them also. If you write down your dream vision and goals, make this as big as you can imagine, nothing is unachievable. When your vision is combined with your inner creativity and drive of passion and love, then you will achieve things you never thought possible and you will be doing for good reasons. This is what will fulfil you, your ability to help others and leave the world better off than when you came into it. Part of my own vision is the ability to help my family, friends and those close to me. The extension of that is helping my wider family, which is those around me and the people I have never met because I understand that everyone on this planet is family on one level or another. We are all connected.

I have always enjoyed helping others, whether that is helping them deal with their issues, overcome negative thinking and behaviour, or inspiring them to go after what really drives them inside. I get a lot of reward and happiness from empathy. I want the best for others because I know what pain is like. Helping others in the right way can be a form of agape by the ancient Greeks. It is a selfless desire to help others and improve the journey of those who you meet. Love for others has helped me overcome my shyness and introversion with public speaking because I would see things from a perspective of wanting to help others before myself. If I kept shy and I didn't speak up, I could not help those around me. I learnt on my journey the value of philautia, which is self-love and acceptance as the initial step in being able to help others.

Some people misunderstand wanting to help yourself and to achieve and become successful as being selfish. This is a view I used to have. I always thought being successful in business meant you had to sacrifice your morals, because in order to get to the top you have to be selfish and trample on people to get there and only through the suffering and defeat of others can you get ahead. I don't know where exactly this belief came from but I think it held me back for a long time because I was brought up and raised to be respectful and courteous to others. It was only when I learnt more about self-development that I began to realise the value of actually helping yourself and that there is nothing wrong with business or getting ahead in life. I see it like so many other things, as an opportunity to develop myself so that I can help others. My success is a good thing because the more I can achieve the more I can help others. This change in perspective allowed me to start thinking bigger and the influence and impact I could have on people in a positive way. I think you are sitting here reading this book now because of that change in perspective. I learnt to embrace the desire to help myself so that I can support my family (storage) and others around me (philia/pragma).

When people say you should "love your job" I like to look at from a slightly different perspective. We can use that phrase as an umbrella term which is perfectly fine but I think what they really mean is that you should love the feelings the job brings. It's not the job but the emotions that drive people, and in particular, the emotions of love through the fun of achievement, adding value to people's lives, creating something worthwhile, or the impact you can have on the community or world; the feelings of self-love, love for family and friends and selfless love is what that they get from following their vision and being in that job. Whatever you do in life, make sure you do it with love and harness its power. Don't be afraid to do it for you, but also try to find a greater purpose as well. Think of how you can excel at what you do so that you can use this talent to benefit others, both close and far, and the world around you.

"When you are inspired by some great purpose, some extraordinary project, all your thoughts break their bounds. Your mind transcends limitations, your consciousness expands in every direction and you find yourself in a new, great and wonderful world. Dormant forces, faculties and talents become alive, and you discover yourself to be a greater person by far than you ever dreamed yourself to be"

Patanjali

"Everyone has been made for some particular work, and the desire for that work has been put in every heart"

Rumi

"I have looked in the mirror every morning and asked myself: 'If today were the last day of my life, would I want to do what I am about to do today?' And whenever the answer has been 'No' for too many days in a row, I know I need to change something"

Steve Jobs

"Yes, I've made a great deal of dough from my fiction, but I never set a single word down on paper with the thought of being paid for it. I have written because it fulfilled me. I did it for the buzz. I did it for the pure joy of the thing. And if you can do it for joy, you can do it forever"

Stephen King

"If it falls your lot to be a street sweeper, go out and sweep streets like Michelangelo painted pictures. Sweep streets like Handel and Beethoven composed music. Sweep streets like Shakespeare wrote poetry. Sweep streets so well that all the hosts of heaven and earth will have to pause and say, here lived a great street sweeper who swept his job well"

Martin Luther King, Jr

"Work is love made visible. And if you cannot work with love but only with distaste, it is better that you should leave your work and sit at the gate of the temple and take alms of those who work with joy"

Kahlil Gibran

"Your work is going to fill a large part of your life, and the only way to be truly satisfied is to do what you believe is great work. And the only way to do great work is to love what you do"

Steve Jobs

"I think people who are creative are the luckiest people on earth. I know that there are no shortcuts, but you must keep your faith in something Greater than You, and keep doing what you love. Do what you love, and you will find the way to get it out to the world"

Judy Collins

"The secret of joy in work is contained in one word: excellence. To know how to do something well is to enjoy it"

Pearl S. Buck

"The law of work seems unfair, but nothing can change it; the more enjoyment you get out of your work, the more money you will make"

Mark Twain

"The people who make it to the top whether they're musicians, or great chefs, or corporate honchos are addicted to their calling. . . are the ones who'd be doing whatever it is they love, even if they weren't being paid"

Quincy Jones

"Never continue in a job you don't enjoy. If you're happy in what you're doing, you'll like yourself, you'll have inner peace. And if you have that, along with physical health, you will have had more success than you could possibly have imagined"

Johnny Carson

"Your work is going to fill a large part of your life, and the only way to be truly satisfied is to do what you believe is great work. And the only way to do great work is to love what you do"

Steve Jobs

"You can only become truly accomplished at something you love. Don't make money your goal. Instead pursue the things you love doing and then do them so well that people can't take their eyes off of you"

Maya Angelou

"When you are inspired by some great purpose, some extraordinary project, all your thoughts break their bounds. Your mind transcends limitations, your consciousness expands in every direction and you find yourself in a new, great and wonderful world. Dormant forces, faculties and talents become alive, and you discover yourself to be a greater person by far than you ever dreamed yourself to be"

Patanjali

"There comes a time when you ought to start doing what you want. Take a job that you love. You will jump out of bed in the morning. I think you are out of your mind if you keep taking jobs that you don't like because you think it will look good on your resume. Isn't that a little like saving up sex for your old age?"

Warren Buffet

"The secret of joy in work is contained in one word: excellence. To know how to do something well is to enjoy it"

Pearl S. Buck

"I have looked in the mirror every morning and asked myself: 'If today were the last day of my life, would I want to do what I am about to do today?' And whenever the answer has been 'No' for too many days in a row, I know I need to change something"

Steve Jobs

"Yes, I've made a great deal of dough from my fiction, but I never set a single word down on paper with the thought of being paid for it … I have written because it fulfilled me. Maybe It paid off the mortgage on the house and got the kids through college, but those things were on the side—I did it for the buzz. I did it for the pure joy of the thing. And if you can do it for the joy, you can do it forever"

Stephen King

"Just don't give up trying to do what you really want to do. Where there is love and inspiration, I don't think you can go wrong"

Ella Fitzgerald

"Everyone has been made for some particular work, and the desire for that work has been put in every heart"

Rumi

"If it falls your lot to be a street sweeper, go out and sweep streets like Michelangelo painted pictures. Sweep streets like Handel and Beethoven composed music. Sweep streets like Shakespeare wrote poetry. Sweep streets so well that all the hosts of heaven and earth will have to pause and say, here lived a great street sweeper who swept his job well"

Martin Luther King, Jr

"I think the foremost quality there's no success without it is really loving what you do. If you love it, you do it well, and there's no success if you don't do well what you're working at"

Malcolm Forbes

"Work is love made visible. And if you cannot work with love but only with distaste, it is better that you should leave your work and sit at the gate of the temple and take alms of those who work with joy"

Kahlil Gibran

"I think people who are creative are the luckiest people on earth. I know that there are no shortcuts, but you must keep your faith in something Greater than You, and keep doing what you love. Do what you love, and you will find the way to get it out to the world"

Judy Collins

"Paul and I, we never thought that we would make much money out of the thing. We just loved writing software"

Bill Gates

"The law of work seems unfair, but nothing can change it; the more enjoyment you get out of your work, the more money you will make"

Mark Twain

"The people who make it to the top whether they're musicians, or great chefs, or corporate honchos are addicted to their calling …. are the ones who'd be doing whatever it is they love, even if they weren't being paid"

Quincy Jones

"Never continue in a job you don't enjoy. If you're happy in what you're doing, you'll like yourself, you'll have inner peace. And if you have that, along with physical health, you will have had more success than you could possibly have imagined"

Johnny Carson

PASSION

Passion is similar to love but there are some subtle differences. Love as we discussed comes in many forms and is mainly to do with the giving and receiving of strong emotions, whether that is giving affection to friends, colleagues and lovers or receiving emotions and rewards such as the emotions that you get from helping others through your work or the feelings of pride and accomplishment. Passion is more concerned with the intense emotions involved in performing the actions themselves. For example, I love the work I do in creating books that help people because this love is often reciprocated in the comments, reviews and stories that I hear through the help I provide. In terms of passions, I have a passion when researching and writing the books because I have a strong and intense desire and I enjoy the hard I put into these books because it stirs up excitement, drive, enthusiasm, fixation and obsession with creating the best work I can possible create.

It is a subtle difference but one worth understanding. Love is the emotions you give or get from something and passion is the emotions you get when doing it. They are often used interchangeably but passion is what pushes us and motivates us daily in achieving great works and love is what pulls us towards the worthy ideal. Passion is energy. Passion is what makes life enjoyable along the way. Purpose and love is the reason you journey, but passion is the fire that lights the way. In an interview with Tony Robbins, he talked about his mum wanting him to join a "Truck Masters" program because he would make twice as much as his father made. He went on to say, "Something inside of me said I don't want to drive a truck, there's something else that matters more to me and I decided that I was not going to go for money instead of passion and the rewards have been pretty amazingly better than being a truck driver, not that there's anything bad with being a truck driver, it was just not what I was after". Tony Robbins went on to be one of the most influential personal development speakers in the world, helping millions of people achieve a better way of living. He has always been one of my own inspirations in life and reinforced my own decision to go after passion and not money. Passion is what helps drive me now and why I enjoy my life and doing what I love. It gives me the energy to work long hours and to work at the weekends.

I talk about how to find and discover your passion in greater detail in my previous book. One of he ways is reflection on your past and looking at the things you really enjoyed doing, like *really* enjoyed. Think about the things that may seem like hard work to others but you enjoyed the passion of working in creating something important to you at that time. It may have been things you done as a child or the things you done in your spare time that you found energy in doing.

Sometimes fear holds you back in following your passion because of doubt, scepticism and critical thinking. These things are important intellectual faculties to have but they are also limits on your mind and your imagination. Through being a visionary and visualising your ideal life with absolutely no thought for *how* you are going to achieve this, you can learn to discover your passions. Your vision must be something so ridiculously out of reach that you barely believe you can do, let alone imagine it. The more you create a detailed fantasies and dream of your ideal life, the more you can start to discover what really drives you and excites you. With an abundance of wealth and money, think about how you would spend your time. That inner desire and passion will start to burn a fire inside you which in turn will help you go out and create that life of your dreams, something of your own, a personal passion to you that will give you a purpose greater than yourself. This is the passion for a worthy ideal that drives people to greater heights and allows them to excel every day.

"Every great dream begins with a dreamer. Always remember, you have within you the strength, the patience, and the passion to reach for the stars to change the world"

Harriet Tubman

"There is no passion to be found playing small in settling for a life that is less than the one you are capable of living"

Nelson Mandela

"Develop a passion for learning. If you do, you will never cease to grow"

Anthony J. D'Angelo

"Passion is energy. Feel the power that comes from focusing on what excites you"

80

Oprah Winfrey

"If passion drives you, let reason hold the reins"

Benjamin Franklin

"We must act out passion before we can feel it"

Jean-Paul Sartre

"It is obvious that we can no more explain a passion to a person who has never experienced it than we can explain light to the blind"

T.S Eliot

"Nothing is as important as passion. No matter what you want to do with your life, be passionate"

Jon Bon Jovi

"You can't fake passion"

Barbara Corcoran

"You have to be burning with an idea, or a problem, or a wrong that you want to right. If you're not passionate enough from the start, you'll never stick it out"

Steve Jobs

"Yes, in all my research, the greatest leaders looked inward and were able to tell a good story with authenticity and passion"

Deepak Chopra

"If you feel like there's something out there that you're supposed to be doing, if you have a passion for it, then stop wishing and just do it"

Wanda Skyes

"If you don't love what you do, you won't do it with much conviction or passion"

Mia Hamm

"It is the soul's duty to be loyal to its own desires. It must abandon itself to its master passion"

Rebecca West

"I have no special talents. I am only passionately curious"

Albert Einstein

"Trust not what inspires other members of society to choose a career. Trust what inspires you"

The Lazy Person's Guide to Success

"You are what you do. If you do boring, stupid, monotonous work, chances are you'll end up boring, stupid, and monotonous"

Bob Black

"I believe you are your work. Don't trade the stuff of your life, time, for nothing more than dollars. That's a rotten bargain"

Rita Mae Brown

"Make no little plans; they have no magic to stir men's blood. Make big plans; aim high in hope and work"

Daniel Burnham

"I'd rather be a failure at something I love than a success at something I hate"

George Burns

"The biggest mistake that you can make is to believe that you are working for somebody else... The driving force of a career must come from the individual. Remember: Jobs are owned by the company, you own your career!"

Earl Nightingale

"Your work is to discover your work and then with all your heart to give yourself to it"

Buddha

"My mother said to me, 'If you become a soldier, you'll be a general, if you become a monk you'll end up as the pope'. Instead, I became a painter and wound up as Picasso"

Pablo Picasso

"Passion will move men beyond themselves, beyond their shortcomings, beyond their failures"

Joseph Campbell

"Any human being is really good at certain things. The problem is that the things you're good at come naturally. And since most people are pretty modest instead of an arrogant S.O.B. like me, what comes naturally, you don't see as a special skill. It's just you. It's what you've always done"

Stephen Jay Gould

"If you don't stand for something, you'll fall for anything"

Michael Evans

"There's nothing in the middle of the road but yellow stripes and dead armadillos"

Jim Hightower

"He who would learn to fly one day must first learn to stand and walk and run and climb and dance; one cannot fly into flying"

Nietzsche

"Desire! That's the one secret of every man's career. Not education. Not being born with hidden talents. Desire"

Bobby Unser

"When you're following your energy and doing what you want all the time, the distinction between work and play dissolves"

Shakti Gawain

"Passion kept one fully in the present, so that time became a series of mutually exclusive 'nows'"

Sue Halpern

FAITH

Faith is the belief in something without evidence (or a lack thereof) and it is having complete trust in someone or something. I am not talking about religious faith here in this section but the concept of faith as defined. I'm would say I'm a pragmatist who is logical, rational and evidence based. For me, faith was a stranger and evidence was my companion. I tried as much as I could to form my decisions based on evidence and gathering up the data. I would think objectively and with my calculated mind I would weigh up the pros and cons. All this type of thinking I still do and it is good and necessary, but it was only recently in my life that I started to understand the concept of faith more and the benefits of it. I came to the realisation through studying that my logical, rational, sceptical, critical thinking mind is also a limiting belief. This struck deep with me but I was quite grateful that someone had enlightened me on the subject. I never realised how much this was holding me back and started trying to understand the limiting beliefs I had involving this. It was through this part of journey that I started harnessing the power of faith and using it as a tool to make big decisions in my life.

Yes, I am still critical and objective, but sometimes all the data just isn't there. In those scenarios it would have brought, doubt, fear and uncertainty and almost all cases it stopped me progressing. I am grateful now that I learnt about faith and how it can be used in decision making and it allows me to focus on what could go right and not on what could go wrong. Most people spend their lives focusing on the negative aspects of decision making, the fears and doubts, instead of focusing on what they could achieve. I remember vividly one day when I had to make a big decision about a very expensive course I was thinking of doing and for days I was dreading the thought of it and what could go wrong and the embarrassment I would face if it didn't work out. Through my practicing of gratefulness and my daily vision exercises that I was doing, it led to my sense of greater awareness which I really feel contributed to the realisation I had.

I woke up, retrieved my notebook and started writing out new affirmations. I wrote down in that notebook that I was going to acknowledge my fears and doubts and trust in the process of the course that it will lead me to greater things. I had barely any evidence that the course was going to work, some mixed reviews and a person who was on the course was all the evidence I had. Logically, sceptically and critically there wasn't enough evidence to support the risk of spending all this money, money I didn't really have to do this course. I decided I was going to have faith and take a leap of faith over a huge chasm of fear and doubt. The course turned out to be one of the best things I've ever done.

I had learned information about faith before from studying self-development and I knew that a leap of faith was the right thing to do. I realised that unless I do what I thought I knew, then I did not really believe it. I decided to have faith in faith. The things I learnt on the course, the like-minded people I met, the mentor and the knowledge I gained was an incredible stepping stone in my own journey in life which propelled me to a better and more enriched life. None of that would ever have been achieved without faith.

Sometimes in life, you just must have faith that things will work out despite the lack of evidence. That belief will help you progress by making risky decisions. Think positive and positive results will follow. Even if things don't go the way you planned, the knowledge, experience and skills you gain along the way is invaluable, so these big risks always pay off anyway. You will never get ahead in life without a certain amount of faith and I learnt that in my own life. My advice, take risks, have faith in your big vision and dreams. Don't worry about how you get there and instead understand that the *how* will come once you have decided to have faith in yourself and in your future. Great things happen when you leap the chasm.

"Believe in yourself! Have faith in your abilities! Without a humble but reasonable confidence in your own powers you cannot be successful or happy"

Norman Vincent Peale

"Take the first step in faith. You don't have to see the whole staircase, just take the first step"

Dr. Martin Luther King Jr.

"I am the greatest. I said that even before I knew I was. Don't tell me I can't do something. Don't tell me it's impossible. Don't tell me I'm not the greatest. I'm the double greatest"

Muhammad Ali

"You can do it if you believe you can!"

Napoleon Hill

"Fear, uncertainty, and doubt are, and always have been, the greatest enemies of success and happiness"

Brian Tracy

"There is a difference between wishing for a thing and being ready to receive it. No one is ready for a thing until they believe they can acquire it. The state of mind must be belief and not mere hope or wish"

Napoleon Hill

"Faith is to believe what you do not see; the reward of this faith is to see what you believe"

Saint Augustine

"You must not lose faith in humanity. Humanity is an ocean; if a few drops of the ocean are dirty, the ocean does not become dirty"

Mahatma Gandhi

"Faith is a living, daring confidence in God's grace, so sure and certain that a man could stake his life on it a thousand times"

Martin Luther

"Faith is the strength by which a shattered world shall emerge into the light"

Helen Keller

"Faith and prayer are the vitamins of the soul; man cannot live in health without them"

Mahalia Jackson

"The principle part of faith is patience"

George MacDonald

"Seeds of faith are always within us; sometimes it takes a crisis to nourish and encourage their growth"

Susan L. Taylor

"Faith is not something to grasp, it is a state to grow into"

Mahatma Gandhi

"Faith gives you an inner strength and a sense of balance and perspective in life"

Gregory Peck

"A man of courage is also full of faith"

Marcus Tullius Cicero

"Worry is spiritual short sight. Its cure is intelligent faith"

Paul Brunton

"As your faith is strengthened you will find that there is no longer the need to have a sense of control, that things will flow as they will, and that you will flow with them, to your great delight and benefit"

Emmanuel Teney

"Keep your dreams alive. Understand to achieve anything requires faith and belief in yourself, vision, hard work, determination, and dedication. Remember all things are possible for those who believe"

Gail Devers

"And above all, watch with glittering eyes the whole world around you because the greatest secrets are always hidden in the most unlikely places. Those who don't believe in magic will never find it"

Roald Dahl

"Sometimes beautiful things come into our lives out of nowhere. We can't always understand them, but we have to trust in them. I know you want to question everything, but sometimes it pays to just have a little faith"
Lauren Kate

"When you get to the end of all the light you know and it's time to step into the darkness of the unknown, faith is knowing that one of two things shall happen: either you will be given something solid to stand on, or you will be taught how to fly"

Edward Teller

"Be believing, be happy, don't get discouraged. Things will work out"

Gordon B. Hinckley

"Faith is an oasis in the heart which will never be reached by the caravan of thinking"

Kahlil Gibran

"Great things happen to those who don't stop believing, trying, learning, and being grateful"

Roy T. Benne

"Believe in a love that is being stored up for you like an inheritance, and have faith that in this love there is a strength and a blessing so large that you can travel as far as you wish without having to step outside it"

Rainer Maria Rilke

"Faith is the bird that feels the light and sings when the dawn is still dark"

Rabindranath Tagore

"All the world is made of faith, and trust, and pixie dust"

J.M. Barrie, Peter Pan

"It is only when we are suspended in mid-air with no landing in sight, that we force our wings to unravel and alas begin our flight. You may not know where you're going, but you know that so long as you spread your wings, the winds will carry you"

C. JoyBell C.

"It does not count if you believe in yourself when it's easy to believe in yourself. […] It counts when it's hard to believe in yourself when it looks like the world's going to end and you've still got a long way to go. That's when it counts. That's when it matters the most"

Iain S. Thoma

"Faithless is he that says farewell when the road darkens"

J.R.R. Tolkien

"Understanding is the reward of faith. Therefore, seek not to understand that you may believe, but believe that you may understand"

Augustine of Hippo

PATIENCE

Today's culture and society makes this one very hard. There is little reinforcement in the world today to encourage this virtue. It's a fast-moving world with instant as the norm. Instant gratification on social media; likes, loves, follows, tweets, live feeds. Let's post the new selfie so we can instantly feel better by getting the validation from others. Instant food through microwaves, instant coffee; latte, cappuccino, non-fat skinny caramel macchiatos. Instant information via the internet, no more having to walk to the library to search for a copy of "Nicomachean Ethics" by Aristotle to find on page 53 the exact quote that I was looking for. Instant movies or TV shows streamed to us to instantly satisfy the urge to watch a horror movie, drama show or mystery movie. Smartphone apps, no more phoning and waiting for taxis just download the latest app and it already knows your location. One-click buy with Amazon because we don't want to click through two more pages, we want to order it now and we want it by tomorrow with Amazon prime.

What's so wrong about this type of culture? Well… absolutely nothing. Providing you don't get sucked into its depths. Who doesn't want instant coffee when you wake up like a zombie because you aren't a morning person and you don't want to walk out the door with your jumper on backwards again. Or who doesn't want to find out the second law of thermodynamics instantly because you have a test tomorrow and you've left it to the last minute to revise. There are obviously lots of benefits to today's fast-moving world but the problem comes when you fall into its deep chasm and forget the value of the long-term work that comes in building something great, the value of being patient through lengthy periods of time because sometimes success is just around the corner, or the value of deeper emotions and connections that comes with patience, perseverance, diligence and persistence. You won't experience philia (deep friendship, comradery, loyalty) or pragma (deep connection between long married couples or relationships) for example, if you don't value the concept of patience.

If you want to be at the pinnacle of your game or endeavour, it will take patience and you will be tested at some point. When you are trying to reach your goal, time will test you to see if you have what it takes to get to your goal. Time will whisper, "this will take too long, try something else", "you have tried for ages, it's time to move on", "hey, what about that other idea, why don't you give that ago". Don't let the gratification monster distract you. Stick to your goals, no matter how long it takes because the sky is always darkest before the dawn.

An early big fitness inspiration of mine Elliot Hulse had a fitness channel and business which took him years to grow. For 5 years, from 2007 to 2013, he constantly pumped out videos daily trying to grow his business with very little results. Then "seemingly overnight" he became a success where his views, channel and business sky rocketed and that launched his Strength Camp business and himself to fame and success in the fitness industry. I use the term "seemingly overnight" because without too much thought you could suppose that because of his one viral video back in 2013, that it launched his career. This term "overnight success" is misleading. As

Elliot Hulse put it, "well if it was an overnight success then it was a 5-year night". The same applies with movie stars that get those lovely titles and sayings, "the movie that launched his career". I guarantee you, that anyone that was an "overnight success" grinded and hustled for years to get to that opportunity where fortune seemed to strike. The point is that overnight success takes years to get. If you want to be successful don't focus on the success, focus on the love and passion for the job and patience and hard work will be the catalyst to launch that career. Develop and nurture this gift through patience and the person you become and the deeper lessons you learn will be far more important. Discover the faith and strength that comes with patience. You will find that success comes as a side effect of patience and hard work.

"I am a great believer in luck. The harder I work, the more of it I seem to have"

Coleman Cox

"A weed is a plant we've found no use for yet"

Ralph Waldo Emerson

"All in good time"

Horace

"Anyone can hold the helm when the sea is calm"
98

Publilius Syrus

"At the bottom of patience, one finds heaven"

Kanuri

"At the gate of patience there is no crowding"

Moroccan

"Bear and forbear"

Unknown

"By diligence and patience, the mouse bit in two the cable"

Ben Franklin

"Don't cross the bridge 'til you come to it"

Henry Wadsworth Longfellow

"Don't cry before you are hurt"

99

Scottish Proverb

"Don't expect things to go right the first time"

Unknown

"Don't halloo until you're out of the wood"

Ben Franklin

"Don't let anyone get your goat"

Unknown

"Don't put the cart before the horse"

John Heywood

"Drive gently over the stones"

Jonathan Swift

"Everything comes to those who wait"

Unknown

"Genius is only a great aptitude for patience"

Georges-Louis Leclerc de Buffon

"God did not create hurry"

Finnish

"Grain by grain a loaf, stone by stone, a castle"

Yugoslavian

"Haste has no blessing"

Swahili

"Haste makes waste"

John Heywood

"Hasty climbers have sudden falls"

Robert Greene

"Keep your shirt on"

American Saying

"Never change horses in midstream"

Abraham Lincoln

"Never cut what can be untied"

Portuguese Proverb

"One step at a time"

Unknown

"Patience is a virtue"

Unknown

"Patience is bitter but its fruit is sweet"

French Proverb

"Patience is the companion of wisdom"

St. Augustine

"The continuous drip polishes the stone"

Peruvian

"The more you ask how much longer it will take, the longer the journey seems"

Maori

"The remedy against bad times is to have patience with them"

Arabic

"The salt of patience seasons everything"

Italian

"What may not be altered is made lighter by patience"

Horace

INSECURITY

This one I have always personally found challenging in particular areas of my own life and I'm going to guess I'm not the only one. It's took me years in some cases to get over some insecurities and some of them still linger around from time to time which I accept and act on despite the insecurities. Just like fear, sometimes you must just accept it and act despite of it. These are areas and opportunities for growth and most insecurities stem from a lack of self-belief and confidence which are only defeated through conquering them. How do we overcome insecurities? Repetition and experience. When we first learnt to drive we were insecure about driving because we didn't have much experience and skill in driving. We overcome this by taking lessons and practicing our skills in the car park and on the roads until we build up our confidence.

It is the same with any areas of insecurity. Another example which we all experience insecurity is dating and relationships. We are scared that things might not work out, we make a fool of ourselves or we will not be good enough. Through repetition of dating and experience as we mature, we learn to gain confidence in his area. We understand that sometimes we may fail or that it may not work out. We also learn that these things do not matter as much as we first thought. Through building up our confidence through repetition and becoming more skilled in this area, we overcome our insecurities. This applies to all insecurities. It is our brain's way of telling us we need to improve in these areas. Some other examples of insecurities are looks, emotions, finances, failures, income or abilities. Many successful people have learned how to overcome these insecurities and they had to go through this process of repetition and gaining experience to gain confidence in that area of their business or life. Repetition and improving skillsets leads to confidence. Don't be afraid to fail over and over until you learn new skills. See it as a process and an opportunity for growth.

Negativity almost always stems from insecurity. People who crave or cannot do something will often chastise someone else because deep down they want what they chastise. They secretly admire or long for those who have or can-do things that they cannot or do the things that they want to do. As Shakespeare put it in King Lear, "The policeman who lashes the whore has a hot need to use her for the very offense for which he plies the lash". Instead of trying to bring others down, lift them up and learn from them and you will soon find yourself climbing up the rope of success. Like the policeman who secretly longs for and suppresses his own desires, understand your own wants and desires and seek first to understand them first and then to overcome them. If you find yourself looking negatively about someone that is confident or skilled, ask yourself what quality do they have that you feel you are lacking in yourself and seek to improve yourself in that area through repetition and acquiring skills through failure and learning.

"A man who goes into a restaurant and blatantly disrespects the servers shows a strong discontent with his own being.

Deep down he knows that restaurant service is the closest thing he will ever experience to being served like a king"

Criss Jami

"A competent and self-confident person is incapable of jealousy in anything. Jealousy is invariably a symptom of neurotic insecurity"

Robert A. Heinlein

"Insecure people only eclipse your sun because they're jealous of your daylight and tired of their dark, starless nights"

Shannon L. Alder

"One of the greatest journeys in life is overcoming insecurity and learning to truly not give a shit"

J.A. Konrath

"The problem with human attraction is not knowing if it will be returned"

Becca Fitzpatrick

"A man's spirit is free, but his pride binds him with chains of suffocation in a prison of his own insecurities"

Jeremy Aldana

"Don't let fear or insecurity stop you from trying new things. Believe in yourself. Do what you love. And most importantly, be kind to others, even if you don't like them"

Stacy London

"A lack of transparency results in distrust and a deep sense of insecurity"

Dalai Lama

"Most bad behaviour comes from insecurity"

Debra Winger

"I never have been insecure, because I see what a waste it is. I know there is a solution to insecurity. I don't tend to be thrown by problems that don't have solutions. And insecurity has a wealth of alternatives"

Drew Barrymore

"The reason we struggle with insecurity is because we compare our behind the scenes with everyone else's highlight reel"

Steve Furtick

"Don't you hate it when people make a joke about you, about something that you are actually incredibly insecure about and they don't realize it, but every laugh feels like a stab in your chest, because it hurts so much and brings up memories you'd rather forget, but you can't say anything, because then people would know your weaknesses. They'd know how insecure you really are. So instead you just laugh it off, and hide the pain you feel inside"

Unknown

"The steps of insecurity: Comparison, Compensation, Competition, Compulsion, Condemnation, Control"

Unknown

"Don't let jealousy fool you. It's just another name for insecurity"

Unknown

"Society taught me that no matter what size I am, I will never be good enough. I'll always be too skinny, too fat, too short, too tall. Too this, too that"

Unknown

"Sometimes I wonder if I will ever be happy with myself. I worry that if I can't be happy with myself, then nobody will ever be happy with me, and that just makes me even more paranoid. It's a cycle, insecurity, unconfident, and diffidence, it's all a cycle and it's destroying me"

Unknown

"No one is perfect. Even the most confident people have insecurities. At some point in of our lives, we may feel we lack something. That is reality. We must try to live as per our capability"

Anil Sinha

"An expectation is a shelter, it gives you a security feeling. So, when someone breaks your expectations he is breaking your shelter, making you insecure, fearful"

Osho

"Humans are strange things. They are the most proud on the outside during the times they are the most insecure on the inside, and they would rather die manipulating others than be brave enough to be honest"

Unknown

"In life, there is always someone out there, who won't like you, for whatever reason, don't let the insecurities in their lives affect yours"

Rashida Rowe

"Pretending to be someone that you are not is hurting yourself. It's telling yourself that the real you is worthless"

Ritu Ghatourey

"Be who you are and say what you feel because those who mind don't matter and those who matter don't mind"

Dr. Seuss

"If anyone tries to pull us down, it goes to show that we're on top of them, so cheer up! Hilarious but true, insecurity reigns in an ugly heart of an empty brain"

Nini

"He who is humble is confident and wise. He who brags is insecure and lacking"

Lisa Edmondson

"I act like sh*t don't phase me, inside it drives me crazy, my insecurities could eat me alive"

Eminem

"If you are insecure, guess what? The rest of the world is, too. Do not overestimate the competition and underestimate yourself. You are better than you think"

Timothy Ferriss

"There can be no security where there is fear"

Felix Frankfurter

"It is when we all play safe that we create a world of utmost insecurity"

Dag Hammarskjold

"The opposite of security is insecurity, and the only way to overcome insecurity is to take risks"

Unknown

"Insecurity is love dressed in a child's clothing"

Kofi Annan

"In a world we find terrifying, we ratify that which doesn't threaten us"

David Mamet

"Without danger, we cannot get beyond danger.... Each one of us requires the spur of insecurity to force us to do our best"

Dr. Harold W. Dodds

"Comparison is the thief of joy"

Teddy Roosevelt

"I have insecurities of course but I don't hang out with anyone who points them out to me"

Adele

"Life is very short. Insecurity is a waste of time"

Diane Von Furstenberg

"Be careful not to mistake insecurity and inadequacy for humility! Humility has nothing to do with the insecure and inadequate! Just like arrogance has nothing to do with greatness!"

C. JoyBell

"We're going to have to let truth scream louder to our souls than the lies that have infected us"

Beth Moore

"I'm not insecure. I've been through way too much f**king sh*t to be insecure. I've got huge balls. But I've been humbled. That makes you grateful for every day you have"

Drew Barrymore

"Your perspective on life comes from the cage you were held captive in"

Shannon L. Alder

"Being different is a revolving door in your life where secure people enter and insecure exit"

Shannon L. Alder

"I'm interested in the fact that the less secure a man is, the more likely he is to have extreme prejudice"

Clint Eastwood

"The enemy uses those things your insecure about. Free yourself and take your power back by being secure in who you are. flaws and all"

Yvonne Pierre

"Insecurity is the worst sense that lovers feel: sometimes the most humdrum desireless marriage seems better. Insecurity twists meanings and poisons trust"

Graham Greene

"Dear insecure girls everywhere, you're not ugly, society is. Sincerely, The truth"

Unknown

"One of the greatest journeys in life is overcoming insecurity and learning to truly not give a s**t"

J.A. Konrath

"We are all beautiful except in the eyes of an insecure"

Unknown

"Anger is a weakness in an insecure personality"

Unknown

"Judging people's flaws will not help justify your own"

Unknown

"Insecurity is an ugly thing, it makes you hate people you don't even know"

Unknown

"Insecurity is self-sabotage. If you want to fly you have to first see your wings"

Unknown

GRATITUDE

Just like in life, I have decided to put gratitude before success in this book. Gratitude should always come before success. There are those who can achieve success without harnessing gratitude, but they never stay there. Sooner or later they fall. If you can't be grateful for what you have today, no matter how much you have tomorrow, it will never be enough. Success is entirely subjective but one things for certain, everyone deep down wants to be happy and this should be a subjective benchmark for success. If you follow the trail of "whys" for what you want then it always comes down to happiness. Those that usually seek happiness through wealth do so because they think when they have enough money to buy that house, to buy that car, to make that first million, then they will be happy. They live in a state of perpetual want. They look constantly to the future and ignore the present, or the state of now, as Eckhart Tolle would say. Happiness only ever exists in the present moment. It is not something you can obtain, it is something that already exists which you can unlock. Part of the process of doing that is gratitude.

Gratitude is something that should be practiced daily and can unlock in yourself a higher awareness. Sounds all spiritual and I suppose that is one way of looking at it. I am a very practical person and when I started applying daily gratitude exercises into my habits it was crazy to see how much my perspective on things changed and how much happier I was and how much I started to notice the positive things around me. It is why you have things like affirmations, yoga, and certain meditation practices. It helps you to connect with the present moment and clear the mind so you can accept the world around you and appreciate it. I started writing down my affirmations and my gratitude list, reading them daily. I wrote down things I am grateful for or I would practice gratitude in my mind. It is so powerful and I will always do this now, for the rest of my life.

New age people would call this operating at a higher vibrational frequency. I started to notice the little things more often, like the sunshine, even on cloudy days if it broke through the clouds for a few seconds and I would be grateful for it. I was grateful for the rain because it waters the plants, trees and vegetation. It allows us to have food and I also love the feeling of the rain on my skin. I was grateful for my family, the friends in my life. I was grateful for my health, the roof over my head, the advancements in medical care. I was grateful for my education and the people who came in and out of my life allowing me to learn and experience things and learn some life lessons. The more I practiced gratitude the more things I noticed that I could be grateful for and the more positive, successful and happier I became and the more I was able to positively influence and uplift the people around me. It was a snowball effect the more I practiced it. Friends, colleagues and family started to be more receptive to me and notice the change in my positive attitude and happiness. It is so powerful which is why it has become a daily routine which I build up through repetition of practice; written, verbally and mentally. Not only can I make myself happy but I can make those around me happier too, which is a great feeling.

"Acknowledging the good that you already have in your life is the foundation for all abundance"

Eckhart Tolle

"If a fellow isn't thankful for what he's got, he isn't likely to be thankful for what he's going to get"

Frank A. Clark

"Feeling gratitude and not expressing it is like wrapping a present and not giving it"

William Arthur Ward

"I would maintain that thanks are the highest form of thought; and that gratitude is happiness doubled by wonder"

G.K. Chesterton

"'Enough' is a feast"

Buddhist proverb

"If you count all your assets, you always show a profit"

Robert Quillen

"Enjoy the little things, for one day you may look back and realize they were the big things"

Robert Brault

"As we express our gratitude, we must never forget that the highest appreciation is not to utter words but to live by them"

John F. Kennedy

"Reflect upon your present blessings, of which every man has plenty; not on your past misfortunes, of which all men have some"

Charles Dickens

"If you want to turn your life around, try thankfulness. It will change your life mightily"

Gerald Good

"Gratitude turns what we have into enough, and more. It turns denial into acceptance, chaos into order, confusion into clarity...it makes sense of our past, brings peace for today, and creates a vision for tomorrow"

Melody Beattie

"The world has enough beautiful mountains and meadows, spectacular skies and serene lakes. It has enough lush forests, flowered fields, and sandy beaches. It has plenty of stars and the promise of a new sunrise and sunset every day. What the world needs more of is people to appreciate and enjoy it"

Michael Josephson

"Gratitude is a currency that we can mint for ourselves, and spend without fear of bankruptcy"

Fred De Witt Van Amburgh

"The way to develop the best that is in a person is by appreciation and encouragement"

Charles Schwab

"He is a wise man who does not grieve for the things which he has not, but rejoices for those which he has"

Epictetus

"At times, our own light goes out and is rekindled by a spark from another person. Each of us has cause to think with deep gratitude of those who have lighted the flame within us"

Albert Schweitzer

"The deepest craving of human nature is the need to be appreciated"

William James

"Be thankful for what you have; you'll end up having more. If you concentrate on what you don't have, you will never, ever have enough"

Oprah Winfrey

"Let us rise up and be thankful, for if we didn't learn a lot today, at least we learned a little, and if we didn't learn a little, at least we didn't get sick, and if we got sick, at least we didn't die; so, let us all be thankful"

Buddha

"Silent gratitude isn't very much to anyone"

Gertrude Stein

"Thankfulness is the beginning of gratitude. Gratitude is the completion of thankfulness. Thankfulness may consist merely of words. Gratitude is shown in acts"

Henri Frederic Amiel

"You cannot do a kindness too soon because you never know how soon it will be too late"

Ralph Waldo Emerson

"When I started counting my blessings, my whole life turned around"

Willie Nelson

"It is impossible to feel grateful and depressed in the same moment"

Naomi Williams

"One can never pay in gratitude; one can only pay 'in kind' somewhere else in life"

Anne Morrow Lindbergh

"Things turn out best for people who make the best of the way things turn out"

John Wooden

"No one who achieves success does so without the help of others. The wise and confident acknowledge this help with gratitude"

Alfred North Whitehead

"Piglet noticed that even though he had a Very Small Heart, it could hold a rather large amount of Gratitude"

A.A. Milne

"Forget yesterday, it has already forgotten you. Don't sweat tomorrow, you haven't even met. Instead, open your eyes and your heart to a truly precious gift, today"

Steve Maraboli

"We should certainly count our blessings, but we should also make our blessings count"

Neal A. Maxwell

"In ordinary life, we hardly realize that we receive a great deal more than we give, and that it is only with gratitude that life becomes rich"

Dietrich Bonhoeffer

"The only people with whom you should try to get even are those who have helped you"

John E. Southard

"I truly believe we can either see the connections, celebrate them, and express gratitude for our blessings, or we can see life as a string of coincidences that have no meaning or connection. For me, I'm going to believe in miracles, celebrate life, rejoice in the views of eternity, and hope my choices will create a positive ripple effect in the lives of others. This is my choice"

Mike Ericksen

"Gratitude also opens your eyes to the limitless potential of the universe, while dissatisfaction closes your eyes to it"

Stephen Richards

"Gratitude and attitude are not challenges; they are choices"

Robert Braathe

"They both seemed to understand that describing it was beyond their powers, the gratitude that spreads through your body when a burden gets lifted, and the sense of homecoming that follows, when you suddenly remember what it feels like to be yourself"

Tom Perrotta

"Gratitude is more of a compliment to yourself than someone else"

Raheel Farooq

"Keep your eyes open and try to catch people in your company doing something right, then praise them for it"

Tom Hopkins

"In life, one has a choice to take one of two paths: to wait for some special dayor to celebrate each special day"

Rasheed Ogunlaru

"This a wonderful day. I've never seen this one before"

Maya Angelou

"Gratitude can transform common days into thanksgivings, turn routine jobs into joy and change ordinary opportunities into blessings"

William Arthur Ward

"Be thankful for what you have; you'll end up having more. If you concentrate on what you don't have, you will never, ever have enough"

Oprah Winfrey

"If a fellow isn't thankful for what he's got, he isn't likely to be thankful for what he's going to get"

Frank A. Clark

"Let gratitude be the pillow upon which you kneel to say your nightly prayer. And let faith be the bridge you build to overcome evil and welcome good"

Maya Angelou

"Cultivate the habit of being grateful for every good thing that comes to you, and to give thanks continuously. And because all things have contributed to your advancement, you should include all things in your gratitude"

Ralph Waldo Emerson

"Gratitude is not only the greatest of virtues, but the parent of all others"

Marcus Tullius Cicero

"The unthankful heart discovers no mercies; but the thankful heart will find, in every hour, some heavenly blessings"

Henry Ward Beecher

"We must find time to stop and thank the people who make a difference in our lives"

John F. Kennedy

"Thank you is the best prayer that anyone could say. I say that one a lot. Thank you expresses extreme gratitude, humility, understanding"

Alice Walker

"None is more impoverished than the one who has no gratitude. Gratitude is a currency that we can mint for ourselves, and spend without fear of bankruptcy"

Fred De Witt Van Amburgh

"Gratitude always comes into play; research shows that people are happier if they are grateful for the positive things in their lives, rather than worrying about what might be missing"

Dan Buettner

"The roots of all goodness lie in the soil of appreciation for goodness"

Dalai Lama

"When I started counting my blessings, my whole life turned around"

Willie Nelson

"Appreciation can change a day, even change a life. Your willingness to put it into words is all that is necessary"

Margaret Cousins

"If you are really thankful, what do you do? You share"

W. Clement Stone

"There are only two ways to live your life. One is as though nothing is a miracle. The other is as though everything is a miracle"

Albert Einstein

"Look at everything as though you were seeing it for the first or the last time, then your time on earth will be filled with glory"

Betty Smith

"When you give and carry out acts of kindness, it's as though something inside your body responds and says, 'Yes, this is how I ought to feel'"

Rabbi Harold Kushner

"Not what we say about our blessings, but how we use them, is the true measure of our thanksgiving"

W.T. Purkiser

"All across America, we gather this week with the people we love to give thanks to God for the blessings in our lives"

President George W. Bush

SUCCESS

Success. What is it? What does it mean to be successful? To answer these, first let's go to the trusty Oxford dictionary to see what the definition is. "Success: The accomplishment of an aim or purpose. Archaic definition: The good or bad outcome of an undertaking". Success is not the acquisition of wealth, our popularity, or the empire we create... unless you define it as that. It is subjective to each person depending on their own aims or purpose. Be very careful how you define success because you may find success does not bring you what you really wanted, what everyone really wants. If you follow the trail of "whys", it always comes down to happiness. Wealth and fame can be a great goal, but it will not bring you fulfilment unless it's coupled with those intangible benefits such as helping others, family, great friends, inner peace, self-love. With the rise of entrepreneurs, there is also a rise in entrepreneurs who have mental health issues or commit suicide.

A study by Dr. Michael Freeman, a clinical professor at UCSF surveyed 242 entrepreneurs. It was one of the first of its kind. Some of the shocking figures showed that 49% of entrepreneurs reported having mental health conditions.

Depression was the number 1 reported condition with 30%, followed by ADHD (29%) and anxiety problems (27%). That's a much higher percentage than the US population in general, where only 7% identified as being depressed. 72% of the immediate family members of entrepreneurs identified with mental health issues.

These are some shocking stats and while I can only give my opinion on this from my own research and knowledge on self-development, I do believe it comes from the attributes that these entrepreneurs assign to their subjective definition of success. It is something to seriously consider for yourself too and something that I am aware of when I created my own definition of success. We are a species that developed altruism and empathy through our evolutionary past to survive. Our social hierarchies and close knit tribal communities greatly prospered through the development of these traits. Whether you look at it from an evolutionary or spiritual stand point, the fact remains that some of the greatest joys in life come from our ability to affect, influence and help others. We live in a symbiotic planet and we are all interconnected on many levels. When defining success always bear this in mind. Set your aims and purpose not just on monetary or material possessions, but on the intangible qualities like family, friends, other people, the environment and all other living animals who inhabit the planet with us.

Have a higher purpose which stems from bettering the world and the people around you. This is not only going to motivate you better for more long-lasting success, but it will bring you rewards and joy far behind the short-lived emotions of driving your Lamborghini or Ferrari. We tend to adapt to our surrounds very quickly which is why we can quickly grow accustomed to lifestyles and material possessions such as driving flashy cars such as Lamborghinis and Ferraris. Shopping addictions are a good example of adapting to surroundings. We love the buzz of buying new clothes but soon after you have worn it a few times, it starts to wear off and you need that dopamine hit through your next shopping experience and wearing a newer outfit.

It's the same principle that applies to material possessions and wealth. You will love your new mansion facing the beach and the ocean, but sooner or later this will wear off and you will become accustomed to it and all you will be left with is the daily annoyance of treading sand into your house and onto the sofa and floors if you have never developed gratitude on your journey to success. The rewards you get from the deeper feelings of helping others and leaving the world better off is a far more rewarding and lasting one. It will give you lasting emotions of pride and inner happiness knowing that you have made a difference.

As you fail over and over on your journey, as you will do because failure is the road to success, remember to keep perspective with helping people along the way. What you see as failure could really be success because if you are helping others then no matter how small it is, you are still making a difference in people's lives, differences and impacts that may seem small to you, but really big in the eyes of those you help. You are still changing someone's life and that makes it all worthwhile. Before I leave you with the final quotes from the book and you continue your journey to success, whatever you have defined that as, I will you give you an excerpt from "The Star Thrower" by Loren Eiseley:

"Once upon a time, there was a wise man who used to go to the ocean to do his writing. He had a habit of walking on the beach before he began his work.

One day, as he was walking along the shore, he looked down the beach and saw a human figure moving like a dancer. He smiled to himself at the thought of someone who would dance to the day, and so, he walked faster to catch up.

As he got closer, he noticed that the figure was that of a young man, and that what he was doing was not dancing at all. The young man was reaching down to the shore, picking up small objects, and throwing them into the ocean.

He came closer still and called out "Good morning! May I ask what it is that you are doing?"

The young man paused, looked up, and replied "Throwing starfish into the ocean."

"I must ask, then, why are you throwing starfish into the ocean?" asked the somewhat startled wise man.

To this, the young man replied, "The sun is up and the tide is going out. If I don't throw them in, they'll die."

Upon hearing this, the wise man commented, "But, young man, do you not realize that there are miles and miles of beach and there are starfish all along every mile? You can't possibly make a difference!"

At this, the young man bent down, picked up yet another starfish, and threw it into the ocean. As it met the water, he said,

"It made a difference for that one."

"Try not to become a man of success. Rather become a man of value"

Albert Einstein

136

"The ones who are crazy enough to think they can change the world, are the ones that do"

Anonymous

"Stop chasing the money and start chasing the passion"

Tony Hsieh

"Success is walking from failure to failure with no loss of enthusiasm"

Winston Churchill

"There are two types of people who will tell you that you cannot make a difference in this world: those who are afraid to try and those who are afraid you will succeed"

Ray Goforth

"Success is not final; failure is not fatal: It is the courage to continue that counts"

Winston S. Churchill

"It is better to fail in originality than to succeed in imitation"

Herman Melville

"The road to success and the road to failure are almost exactly the same"

Colin R. Davis

"Success usually comes to those who are too busy to be looking for it"

Henry David Thoreau

"Opportunities don't happen. You create them"

Chris Grosser

"Don't be afraid to give up the good to go for the great"

John D. Rockefeller

"I find that the harder I work, the more luck I seem to have"

Thomas Jefferson

"Successful people do what unsuccessful people are not willing to do. Don't wish it were easier; wish you were better"

Jim Rohn

"Never give in except to convictions of honor and good sense"

Winston Churchill

"I owe my success to having listened respectfully to the very best advice, and then going away and doing the exact opposite"

G. K. Chesterton

"Would you like me to give you a formula for success? It's quite simple, really: Double your rate of failure. You are thinking of failure as the enemy of success. But it isn't at all. You can be discouraged by failure or you can learn from it, so go ahead and make mistakes. Make all you can. Because remember that's where you will find success"

Thomas J. Watson

"If you are not willing to risk the usual, you will have to settle for the ordinary"

Jim Rohn

"Do one thing every day that scares you"

Anonymous

"All progress takes place outside the comfort zone"

Michael John Bobak

"People who succeed have momentum. The more they succeed, the more they want to succeed, and the more they find a way to succeed. Similarly, when someone is failing, the tendency is to get on a downward spiral that can even become a self-fulfilling prophecy"

Tony Robbins

"Don't let the fear of losing be greater than the excitement of winning"

Robert Kiyosaki

"If you really look closely, most overnight successes took a long time"

Steve Jobs

"The real test is not whether you avoid this failure, because you won't. It's whether you let it harden or shame you into inaction, or whether you learn from it; whether you choose to persevere"

Barack Obama

"The only limit to our realization of tomorrow will be our doubts of today"

Franklin D. Roosevelt

"Character cannot be developed in ease and quiet. Only through experience of trial and suffering can the soul be strengthened, ambition inspired, and success achieved"

Helen Keller

"The way to get started is to quit talking and begin doing"

Walt Disney

"The successful warrior is the average man, with laserlike focus"

Bruce Lee

"There are no secrets to success. It is the result of preparation, hard work, and learning from failure"

Colin Powell

"Success seems to be connected with action. Successful people keep moving. They make mistakes, but they don't quit"

Conrad Hilton

"If you really want to do something, you'll find a way. If you don't, you'll find an excuse"

Jim Rohn

"I cannot give you the formula for success, but I can give you the formula for failureIt is: Try to please everybody"

Herbert Bayard Swope

"Success is not the key to happiness. Happiness is the key to success. If you love what you are doing, you will be successful"

Albert Schweitzer

"Success isn't just about what you accomplish in your life; it's about what you inspire others to do"

Unknown

"Fall seven times and stand up eight"

Japanese Proverb

"Some people dream of success while others wake up and work"

Unknown

"If you can dream it, you can do it"

Walt Disney

"The difference between who you are and who you want to be is what you do"

Unknown

"A successful man is one who can lay a firm foundation with the bricks that other throw at him"

David Brinkley

"In order to succeed, your desire for success should be greater than your fear of failure"

Bill Cosby

"In order to succeed, we must first believe that we can"

Nikos Kazantzakis

"Many of life's failures are people who did not realize how close they were to success when they gave up"

Thomas Edison

"Don't be distracted by criticism. Rememberthe only taste of success some people get is to take a bite out of you"

Zig Ziglar

"The secret of success is to do the common thing uncommonly well"

John D. Rockefeller Jr.

"You know you are on the road to success if you would do your job, and not be paid for it"

Oprah Winfrey

"There is a powerful driving force inside every human being that, once unleashed, can make any vision, dream, or desire a reality"

Anthony Robbins

"The secret to success is to know something nobody else knows"

Aristotle Onassis

"I failed my way to success"

Thomas Edison

"I never dreamed about success, I worked for it"

Estee Lauder

"I never did anything worth doing by accident, nor did any of my inventions come indirectly through accident, except the phonograph. No, when I have fully decided that a result is worth getting, I go about it, and make trial after trial, until it comes"

Thomas Edison

"The only place where success comes before work is in the dictionary"

Vidal Sassoon

"Keep on going, and the chances are that you will stumble on something, perhaps when you are least expecting it. I never heard of anyone ever stumbling on something sitting down"

Charles F. Kettering

CONCLUSION

I will go back to where it all begin in this book and that is virtues and characteristics. Develop your character and change yourself as a person through challenges and adversity to become a stronger person. If you do this, I guarantee the world around you will start to change too. Understand and learn more about traits and characteristics to give you the understanding and strength to start practicing these qualities. The importance is on practicing and acting upon them. Like Aristotle said, "We are not studying in order to know what virtue is, but to become good, for otherwise there would be no profit in it".

Now that you understand success and its subjective and personal meaning, seek to visualize and go after what you want in life through setting the right aims and purpose to that vision of success. You are now equipped with some of the knowledge and qualities from some of the greatest minds in human history and have learnt about those characteristics, virtues and qualities and why they are important. Characteristics, virtues and qualities that these great men and women possessed which helped them excel in life. There is no completion in life so continually seek to improve yourself and spend your time wisely through the acquisition of knowledge and more importantly, the practicing of this knowledge. My own journey continues and I am always learning and growing and I enjoy all of it, being grateful for where I am and excited about where I have still yet to go. I will leave you with one final quote from another inspiration of mine which I think is rather fitting to end with.

"Knowing is not enough, we must apply. Willing is not enough, we must do."

Bruce Lee

Thanks for reading "Positive Thinking Positive Life: 365 Quotes".
I hope to see you again soon for some more of my popular Positive Thinking books.

If you enjoyed this book or found it useful, please show your support by leaving a review or by clicking on the link below (e-book only):

Thank you for reading

We invite you to share your thoughts and reactions

amazon

+Add to
goodreads

Pin it

First Printing, 2017

ISBN: 9781549844294

Top10 Publishing

123 Oval Road

London, NW1 7EA

25503462R00083

Printed in Great Britain
by Amazon